# Knots

## useful and ornamental

### Table of Contents

| | |
|---|---|
| ty Bag Lanyard . . . . . . . . . . . 3 | Ringbolt Hitching or Cockscombing . . . 23 |
| hipmaker's Cracker Twist . . . . . . . 5 | Single Strand Cockscombing . . . . . 23 |
| l Mathew Walker, multiple strands . . . 5 | Thump Mat . . . . . . . . . . . . 24 |
| athew Walker Knot . . . . . . . . . 6 | Rope Mat using Prolong Knot . . . . . 25 |
| ll Mathew Walker Knot . . . . . . . . 6 | Extending the Prolong Knot . . . . . 26 |
| Plait, round . . . . . . . . . . . . . 7 | Enlarging a Rope Mat Quickly . . . . 26 |
| ernate Strand Wall Knot . . . . . . . 7 | GENERAL KNOTS . . . . . . . . 26 |
| Strand Crown Sinnet . . . . . . . . . 8 | Thumb Knot . . . . . . . . . . . . 26 |
| Strand Square Sinnet . . . . . . . . . 8 | Figure of Eight . . . . . . . . . . . 26 |
| Part, 5 Bight Turk's-head . . . . . . . . 9 | Reef Knot . . . . . . . . . . . . . 27 |
| Plait, round . . . . . . . . . . . . . 9 | Sheet Bend . . . . . . . . . . . . 27 |
| ternat Crown Sinnet . . . . . . . . 10 | Fisherman's Knot . . . . . . . . . 27 |
| all Knot . . . . . . . . . . . . . . 10 | Timber Hitch . . . . . . . . . . . 27 |
| ll Ropes . . . . . . . . . . . . . 11 | Clove Hitch . . . . . . . . . . . . 28 |
| iamond Knot . . . . . . . . . . . 12 | Constrictor Knot . . . . . . . . . . 28 |
| ezing and Stopping . . . . . . . . 12 | Sheepshank . . . . . . . . . . . . 29 |
| mplified 8 Plait (round) . . . . . . . 12 | Carrier's Knot . . . . . . . . . . . 29 |
| oubled 4 Plait . . . . . . . . . . . 13 | Two Half Hitches . . . . . . . . . 30 |
| opper Knot . . . . . . . . . . . . 13 | Ladder Hitch . . . . . . . . . . . 30 |
| Strand Knob . . . . . . . . . . . . 14 | Ring Hitch . . . . . . . . . . . . 30 |
| panish Ring Knot . . . . . . . . . . 15 | Quick Release Knot . . . . . . . . 31 |
| ey Ring Holder . . . . . . . . . . 15 | Slipped Buntline Hitch . . . . . . . 31 |
| nprovised Bell Rope . . . . . . . . 15 | Fishing Hook Knots . . . . . . . . 31 |
| eaving Line Knot . . . . . . . . . 16 | Mesh Knot . . . . . . . . . . . . 32 |
| onkey's Fist . . . . . . . . . . . . 17 | Bowline . . . . . . . . . . . . . 32 |
| anrope Knot . . . . . . . . . . . 18 | Honda Knot . . . . . . . . . . . . 32 |
| nkle Bracelet . . . . . . . . . . . 19 | Hangman's Noose . . . . . . . . . 33 |
| lass Coaster . . . . . . . . . . . . 20 | Common Whipping . . . . . . . . 33 |
| hort Prolong Knot . . . . . . . . . 20 | Long Whipping . . . . . . . . . . 33 |
| Part 5 Bight Turk's-head . . . . . . . 20 | Eye Splice . . . . . . . . . . . . 34 |
| Part 4 Bight Turk's-head . . . . . . . 21 | Eye Splice in the Bight . . . . . . . 35 |
| Carrick Bend . . . . . . . . . . . 21 | Fast Eye Splice . . . . . . . . . . 35 |
| tar Knot . . . . . . . . . . . . . 22 | Back Splice+ . . . . . . . . . . . 36 |
| Becket . . . . . . . . . . . . . . 22 | Common Splice . . . . . . . . . . 36 |

*Copyright © Ron Edwards 1993*
**The Rams Skull Press**
12 Fairyland Rd
Kuranda, Qld 4872
Australia

Conrad's 'OTAGO'

# Alphabetical Index

Alternate Crown Sinnet 10
Alternate Strand Wall Knot 7
Ankle Bracelet 19
Back Splice+ 36
Becket 22
Bell Ropes 11,15
Bowline 32
Buntline Hitch, slipped 31
Carrick Bend 21
Carrier's Knot 29
Clove Hitch 28
Coaster 20
Cockscombing 23
Common Splice 36
Common Whipping 33
Constrictor Knot 28
Crown sinnet, alternate 10
Crown sinnet, 8 strand 8
Diamond Knot 12
Ditty Bag Lanyard 3
Doubled 4 Plait 13
Enlarging a Rope Mat Quickly 26
Extending the Prolong Knot 26
Eye Splice, Fast 35
Eye Splice in the Bight 35
Eye Splice 34
Figure of Eight Knot 26
Fisherman's Knot 27
Fishing Hook Knots 31
Fishing Net Knot 32
Full Mathew Walker Knot 5,6
Full Mathew Walker, multiple strands 5
General Purpose Knots 26-33
Glass Coaster 20
Half Hitches, two 30
Hangman's Noose 33
Heaving Line Knot 16
Honda Knot 32
Improvised Bell Rope 15
Key Ring Holder 15
Knob knot, 8 strand 14
KNOTS, GENERAL PURPOSE 26-33
Ladder Hitch 30
Lanyard 3
Lasso Knot 32
Long Whipping 33

Manrope Knot 18
Mathew Walker Knot 6
Mesh Knot 32
Monkey's Fist 17
Net Knot 32
3 Part, 5 Bight Turk's-head 9
Plaiting, 4 plait, doubled 13
Plaiting, round 8 plait 7
Plaiting, round 8 plait, simplified 12
Plaiting, round 4 plait 9
8 Plait, round 7
4 Plait, round 9
Quick Release Knot 31
Reef Knot 27
Ringbolt Hitching 23
Ring Hitch 30
Ring Knot, Spanish 15
Rope mats 20,24,25,26
Rope Mat using Prolong Knot 25
Sheepshank 29
Sheet Bend 27
Short Prolong Knot 20
Siezing and Stopping 12
Simplified 8 Plait (round) 12
Single Strand Cockscombing 23
Sinnet 8 Strand Crown 8
Slipped Buntline Hitch 31
Spanish Ring Knot 15
Splices 34,35,36
Square Sinnet, 8 Strand 8
Star Knot 22
Stopper Knot 13
8 Strand Knob 14
Thumb Knot 26
Thump Mat 24
Timber Hitch 27
Turk's-head, 3 part, 5 bight 9
Turk's-head, 3 Part 4 Bight 21
Turk's-head, 3 Part 5 Bight 20
Turk's-head used as ankle bracelet 19
Two Half Hitches 30
Wall Knot, alternate strand 7
Wall Knot 10
Whipmaker's Cracker Twist 5
Whipping 33

# The Sea and Ships

**Ditty Bag Lanyard**

The old sailor's ditty bag was a small bag used to store personal items, and he also had a large bag for clothes. This was later adopted by the armed forces and known as a kit bag. It is sometimes called a sausage bag because of its shape, and is a convenient way to carry clothing.

Unlike a suitcase the bag takes up only as much space as the contents inside it, and it can be packed away into all sorts of odd corners when space is short. This sort of bag is good for camping because it takes up less space in the vehicle.

Ditty bags usually had a number of eyelets around the mouth and cords were attached to these so that the bag could be closed up and also hung up out of the way.

The lanyard which formed one end of these cords was the perfect place for the sailor to display his knowledge of fancy knots, and so demonstrate his skill as a seaman.

In *Bushcraft 1* page 71 I have illustrated a simple lanyard using only four patterns, but this present one is much more elaborate and displays quite a range of techniques.

It belonged to my sister-in-law Pam Edwards, and was made by her grandfather Hugh Dunlop who was born in 1853 and sent to sea at the age of 9. It was while serving under sail that he made this lanyard, some time before 1886. It appeared to have been made from cream coloured linen cord and was still in perfect order after more than a hundred years when I came to draw it in 1993.

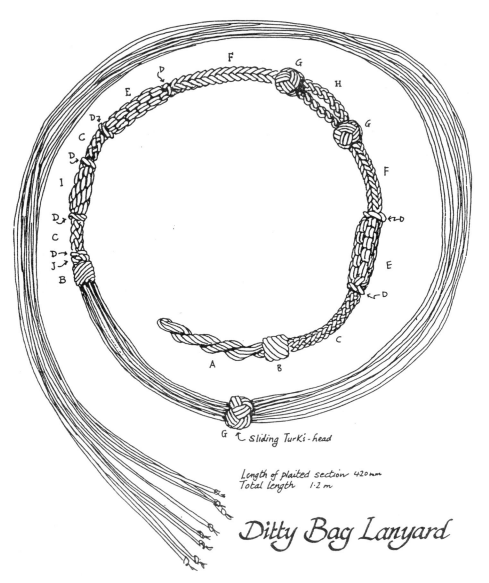

Sliding Turk's-head

Length of plaited section 420 mm
Total length 1.2 m

# Ditty Bag Lanyard

Ten designs are used as follows.
A. Whipmaker's Cracker Twist.
B. Mathew Walker Knot.
C. 8 Plait, round.
D. Alternate Strand Wall Knot.
E. 8 Strand Crown Sinnet.
F. 8 Strand Square Sinnet.
G. 3 Part, 5 Bight Turk's-head.
H. A pair of 4 Plaits.
I. Alternate Crown Sinnet.
J. Wall Knot.

The 3 part 5 bight Turk's-head appears three times. In two cases it is tightly worked onto the lanyard and is a fixture, but the third one is loose and slides up and down the cords and so acts to close the mouth of the ditty bag. This Turk's-head is explained in *Bushcraft 1* Page 71, but I have also reproduced it here for the benefit of those who do not have that book.

**Whipmaker's Cracker Twist**

I do not know what the old sailors called this twist, but it is the same one that is used to make crackers for whips. The strands are grasped firmly and twisted in opposite directions until they begin to kink. At this point they will be found to twist around each other easily and once this has been done they will remain permanently in this shape.

**Full Mathew Walker, multiple strands**

The full Mathew Walker can be done with any number of strands, and here I have used 8. If this gives you trouble then practise first with the three strand version on the next page.

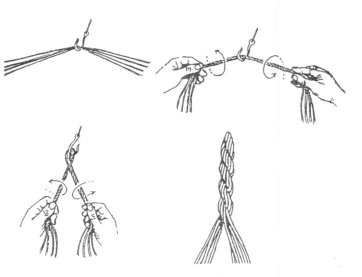

Although the method is simple the Mathew Walker Knot can be a problem to form neatly unless you keep everything in order as you go. Each loop should sit neatly next to the last one.

First tie the previous work together with a bit of thread, this can be removed later if you wish.

Start with a loop that is large enough to be able to take all the 8 strands.

Figure 3 shows how the thumb is used to hold the loops neatly in place.

Figure 4 shows the fourth strand being put in place and the dotted arrow shows the next one to go. Select the strands in order as they go round the circumference of the bundle rather than picking them up at random.

Figure 5 shows all the strands in place.

Figure 6 shows how the last loop is now carefully moved across and tightened up.

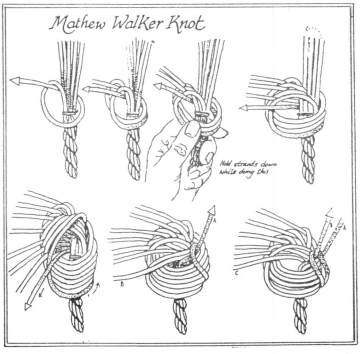

The last figure shows how the same is done with the next strand and so on until all the strands have been moved and tightened. Carefully work it into the final shape, tugging and pulling will not get it right. It might take two or three goes before you get the hang of it.

When finished it should look like this.

## Mathew Walker Knot

An old manual of seamanship once stated "Amongst knots proper the Mathew Walker is almost the only one which is absolutely necessary for the seaman to know", and the knotting expert Ashley noted "It is the most important knot used aboard ship" (Ashley #681). Yet today few people seem to know it, and in fact few seafarers seem to bother about putting stopper knots at the end of their ropes.

No one knows who Mathew Walker was, but the legend has it that he was a Master Rigger who was once sentenced to severe punishment. He made a bargain with the Captain that if he could tie a knot that the other could neither tie or untie then he would be let go free.

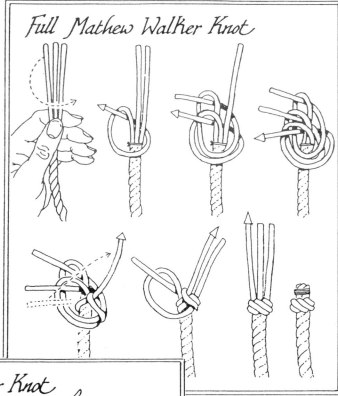

He then took a long length of rope and in private unlaid it halfway, put in one of these knots and then laid it up again. As no one could work out how the knot had been formed in the centre of the rope he was released.

### Full Mathew Walker Knot
This is thought to be the original form, done with three strands of the rope. When completed the ends are whipped.

### Mathew Walker Knot
This is a later knot which Ashley noted as having become more popular than the original one so that it too is often called the Mathew Walker knot. Form a wall knot as shown in the first 4 steps and then work it into the final form, whipping the end.

## 8 Plait, round

This is a simple under one - over one sequence but when done in cord it is not a very attractive looking weave to my eyes. A simplified 8 plait is shown a few pages on which is faster to do. This regular version works better with flat material such as kangaroo lace and looks quite good when worked into a whip handle.

The first three drawings show how to begin the plait so that there will not be a gap at the start, the rest of the drawings show how the normal plaiting pattern goes. In each case the top strand is taken around the back of the work and then follows the pattern shown.

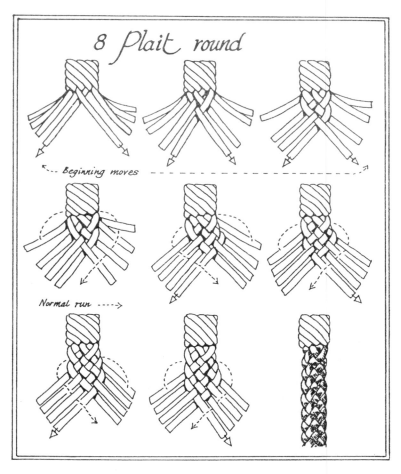

## Alternate Strand Wall Knot

Before attempting this have a look at the normal Wall Knot, which is a few pages on. With the normal Wall Knot every strand is picked up in turn, but with this one each second strand is ignored.

The purpose of this knot is partly for decoration but mainly to get all the strands neatly together so that you can begin the next sequence.

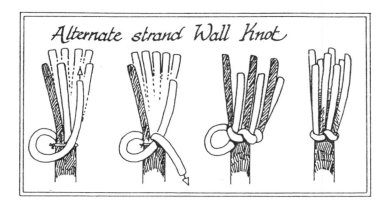

## 8 Strand Crown Sinnet

This is only a variation of the ordinary Crown Knot. However in this case the strands are arranged in pairs as shown in the first drawing. Figures 2 - 5 show how the first section of the knot is formed. The final drawing shows the start of the next sequence.

As you continue to tie this knot an unusual square section is formed with a distinctive pattern as shown.

## 8 Strand Square Sinnet

Anyone who has made whips will recognise this as the Cowtail, or Whipmaker's Plait. The strange thing about it is that when it is formed with flat kangaroo lace around a whip belly it forms a perfectly round section, but when it is formed in cord without a belly it comes out with a square section as shown.

The first four drawings show how to start the plait in order to avoid a gap at the front. The last four drawings show the normal run of the plait, which consists of taking the top strand around the back and then under two - over two.

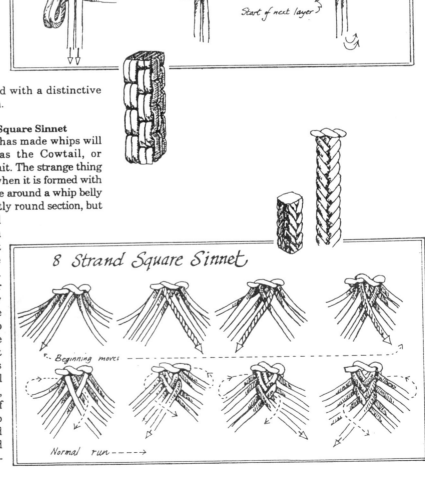

### 3 Part, 5 Bight Turk's-head

This is best formed on the fingers and then transferred to the job where it is tightened up (though of course you can also form it directly on the job if you wish).

To avoid wasting cord you can leave the roll of cord still attached as indicated in the first drawing.

Figure D shows the back of the hand with the two strands pulled across each other to make hole through which to thread the end of the cord.

When you get to figure G the knot is complete. Now you follow round two or three times as desired in order to make the final shape of the knot.

This is where it is convenient to still have the roll of thread attached as this following around can be done from either end. When completed the Turk's-head is tightened up on the job and the ends trimmed off neatly

### 4 Plait

The next section of the lanyard illustrated earlier may look complicated but it is nothing more than a pair of four plaits. This creates a loop, and this was probably used to hang up the ditty bag as it would not be inconvenient to open up a loop in the twisted section at the very start of the lanyard every time you wished to hang it up.

The eight strands are first tied together with a scrap of thread. They are then halved and the two sections of 4 plait worked. When this is finished the two parts are again tied together with thread.

Both of these tied sections are later covered with the Turk's-heads, and this would normally be done at the end of the job.

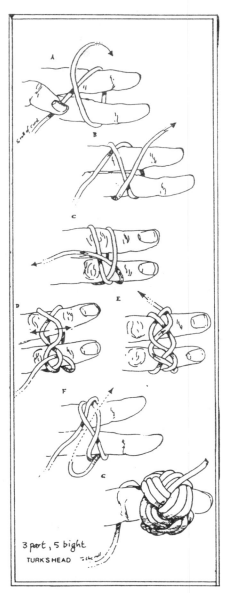

3 part, 5 bight TURK'S HEAD

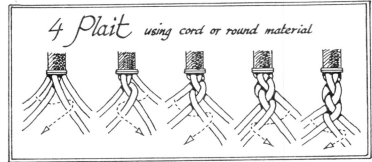

4 Plait using cord or round material

### Alternate Crown Sinnet

This is simple enough to do, but you must tighten it up very evenly after each round in order to end up with a neat, firm job.

The three drawings show how the first round is formed, and this is repeated as often as desired in order to make the required length.

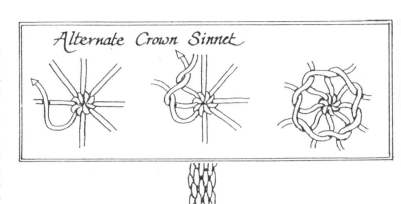

### Wall Knot

Towards the end of the lanyard you will see that an Alternate Strand Wall Knot is formed and then right next to it is an ordinary Wall Knot. This has been done in order to get all the strands neatly together for the final Mathew Walker Knot which concludes this section of the lanyard.

The Wall Knot is a well known one and is used as part of a number of stopper knots. For instance the Crown Knot (explained earlier) is often combined with a Wall Knot, the ends of which are then pushed up through the centre of the Crown Knot to form a permanent stopper knot.

However in this case a Mathew Walker Knot is formed. From here the strands go out and are attached to eyelets in the bag. A Turk's-head, the same as those used earlier,

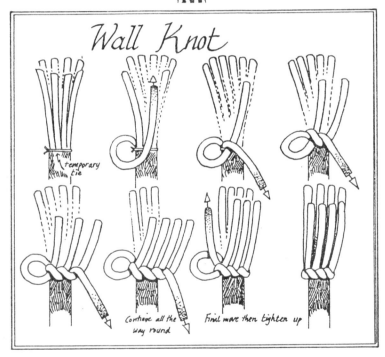

slides up and down in order to close up the mouth of the bag.

This bag can be of any dimensions that you like. The clothes bag in the sketch at the beginning was 900mm long and 750mm in circumference, made of light canvas, and with 8 brass eyelets.

*Golden Plover*

## BELL ROPES

One old bit of seafaring lore that old salts often spring on newcomers is that there is only one rope on a ship, and that is the bell rope. All the other cordage has its own special names, sheets, halyards, etc. (However Bill Scott tells me that in the Australian Navy there were two ropes, the second one being the boat rope).

Like ditty bag lanyards the bell rope was also one of the features which the skilled seaman could decorate with a variety of different knots.

In 1993 while sailing on the old brigantine *Golden Plover* I made new ropes for both the bow and stern bells, and these are illustrated here. The central and shorter rope was made for another ship's bell.

Many of the knots have already been ilustrated in the previous section, and the rest are featured here.

The ropes were made from 3.17mm diameter nylon venetian blind cord which was carried on the ship for a variety of small jobs.

The two longer bell ropes begin with a 4 plait which is then brought together to create 8 strands, each of which should be just over a metre long. The final bell rope will be under 500mm. Begin with 4 strands each 2.5 metres long and double these over to make 8 strands each 1.25 metres long. This will leave you with some waste at the end, but it is better to have some over than not have enough to work the final knob. The knots used are as follows:

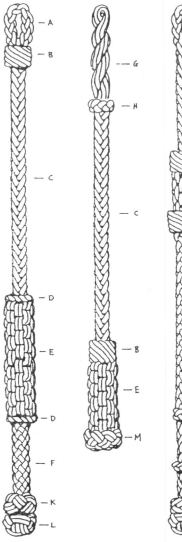

A. 4 plait.
B. Full Mathew Walker Knot.
C. 8 strand Square Sinnet.
D. Wall Knot.
E. 8 strand Square Sinnet.
F. 8 strand Round Plait.
G. Whipmaker's Cracker Twist.
H. Diamond Knot.
I. Simplified 8 Plait.
J. Doubled 4 Plait.
K. 3 part 5 bight Turk's Head.
L. A Stopper Knot.
M. 8 Strand Knob.
N. Spanish Ring Knot.

## Diamond Knot

This is a neat small knot which is easy to do if you put on a temporary tie as is shown in the second drawing. Skilled plaiters can tie it without the temporary tie, but this takes practise. It can be tied with any number of strands, and you may like to start by trying it out with some three strand rope. It is a very old knot and Ashley notes a mention of it dating back to 1769 (Ashley #683).

The ends are placed as in the 3rd and 4th drawing, and this is then continued all the way round until it looks like figure 5. This is then tightened up and the end is whipped, or you may go onto a new pattern.

## Siezing and Stopping

When talking about the diamond knot Ashley, the knot expert, said that the rope is first siezed, as shown in the first figure and then it is next stopped, as in the second figure. The difference is that a siezing is meant to be permanent, while a stop, even though it may be tied in the same way, is intended to be removed later.

## Simplified 8 Plait (round)

This is a little faster and easier to do than the ordinary 8 plait shown earlier, and to my mind it looks better when done in cord, even though in fact the design is irregular, being different on the back to the front.

The sequence on both the left and right sides is *under 1 - over 2 - under 1*.

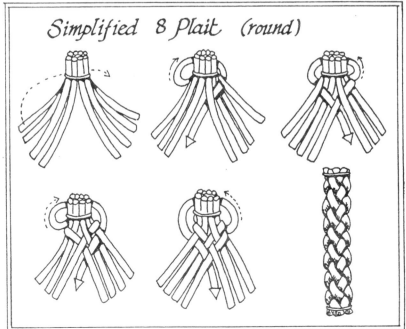

**Doubled 4 Plait**

This looks quite good and yet is nothing more than an ordinary 4 plait worked with two strands at a time instead of one. I illustrated this being used for very large ship's rope in *Bush Leatherwork*.

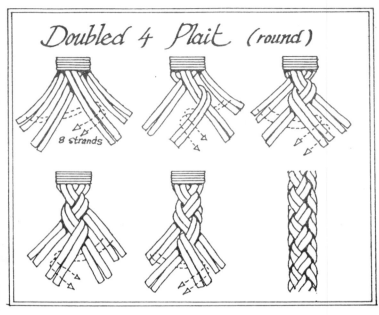

**A Stopper Knot**

Stopper knots are used when you want a knob on the end of a rope. There are lots of varieties of stopper knots, many of which are quite hard to do. This one has the advantage of being fairly simple and will work with the 8 strands in the bell rope.

Before working on this sort of knot you must be familiar with both the Wall Knot and the Crown Knot, as they are used in most of these stopper knots. They are described earlier in detail, but here I have just shown them complete.

You make a Crown, then a Wall and then another Crown. The ends are then tucked in as shown in the fourth drawing and the knot is complete.

The ends can then be whipped or covered with a Spanish Ring Knot or even a 3 part 5 bight Turk's-head (shown earlier).

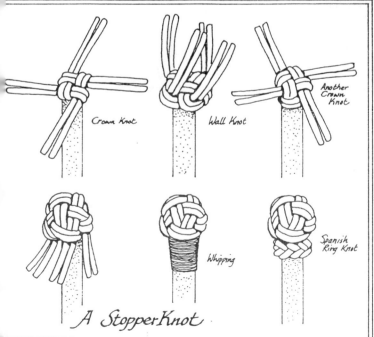

**8 Strand Knob**

According to the experts this is not a Turk's-head, even though it looks like one, because a true Turk's-head is made from a single length of material while this is made from multiple strands.

It is not a difficult knot to do, once you understand the principles, but it is a slow one to tighten up because each strand in the pair is going in the opposite direction to its neighbour. This may be hard to understand at first reading, but after you have tried it you will realise what I mean.

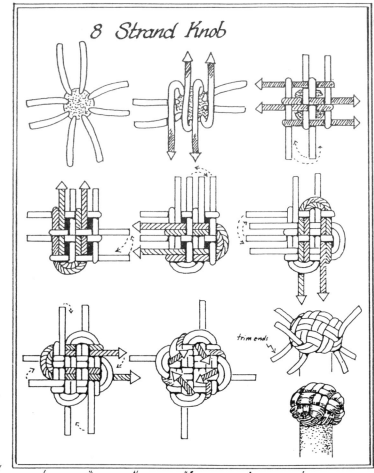

**Spanish Ring Knot**

I have described this elsewhere. It is a common knot among many whipmakers but not seen so much worked in cord. It begins with the 3 part 5 bight Turk's-head shown earlier and can be tied on the fingers in the same way.

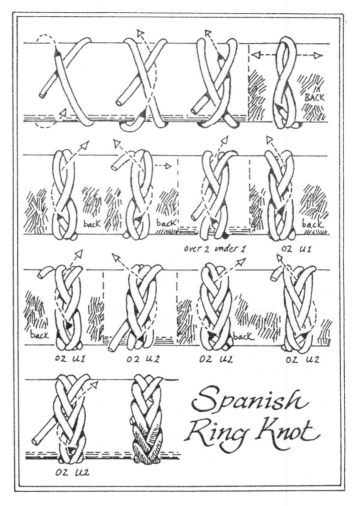

**Key Ring Holder**

The above knots can be used for all sorts of jobs, for instance this key ring holder is made from venetian blind cord and is just the same as a small bell rope. From the top the knots are - 4 plait for the loop, Diamond Knot, 8 strand Square Sinnet, Diamond Knot, 8 strand Crown Sinnet, 8 strand Knob.

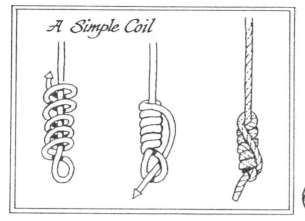

### Improvised Bell Rope

The fancy patterns on the traditional bell ropes on sailing ships were not only decorative, but they did have one practical purpose, and that was to provide a sure grip when the rope was wet. Their bulk also stopped the rope blowing about.

This is the rather plain forward bell rope on the *Golden Plover* that the skipper asked me to replace, but before doing so I did a sketch as the sails were being loosened.

This simple coil did the job, and was a quick solution of the problem of providing a hand grip. However the next knot would have been a bit neater.

### Heaving Line Knot

This would have provided a neat grip on the bell rope described above, but its original

purpose, as the name suggests, was to provide some weight on the end of a line that was being thrown ashore or to another vessel. This however was only a makeshift solution to the problem and most vessels carried a heaving line with a proper monkey's fist on it as is described next.

### Monkey's Fist

This is worked permanently into the end of the heaving line, a light line which is thrown ashore or to another vessel, and to which a heavier rope can then be attached once the link has been made. Fortunately the Monkey's Fist is easy to make, because nearly every vessel has one. There are complex diagrams showing how to do it in some manuals, but old sailors work it around their fingers as shown.

The cord is taken round in three directions as shown and then a small marble or round stone is placed inside and the whole thing is tightened up. The knotting expert Ashley noted that there were sporting limits to the size of the ball put into the knot - it would be easy to knock a person out with a badly aimed throw if the weight was too heavy!

Large marbles are often used because round stones are harder to find than you may think. The one in my sketch was picked up near Gawler, South Australia, at a place called Dead Man's Pass. I thought that it was unusual at the time, and later found similar stones on view at the Kapunda Museum where they were described as emu stones.

These are stones that emus swallow and which

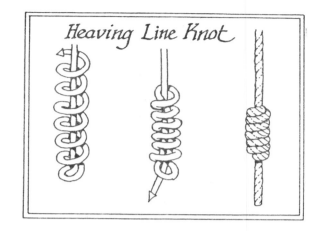

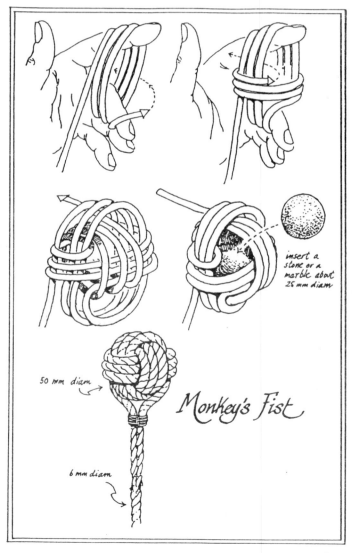

remain inside them all their lives and help grind up their food. In the course of this constant movement the stones end up as perfect spheres.

**Manrope Knot**

Manrope knots used to be tied into the end of the length of rope to provide a handhold to anyone who had to grab it. Ashley notes it as being used on ropes near the gangway on a ship and also to provide a handhold to anyone climbing the side ladder. He also notes "A man who can make a Manrope Knot, Star Knot or Rose Knot is an object of respect" (Ashley #847).

There are a number of versions of this knot, and this is one of the easier ones. As with the Stopper Knot you have to be able to tie both a Wall Knot and a Crown Knot before you begin working with these more complicated knots.

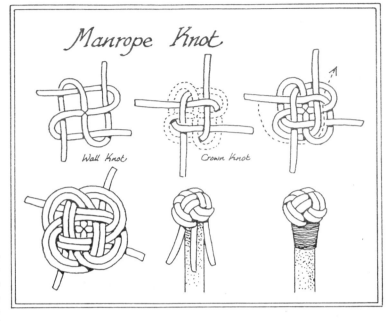

You will note that it begins with four strands. Begin with a Wall Knot. Take the ends and form a Crown Knot (the original Wall Knot is shown in the second drawing with dotted lines so that the new knot is easier to see). The third drawing shows how the end is lead around following a previous strand, but notice that at the end it comes out *below* the final crossing and not above it as does the strand to its left.

All the ends are treated in the same way until you should end up with a patttern like the fourth drawing. This is then carefully worked tight to form a ball and the ends are then whipped (or they can be concealed under a Spanish Ring Knot as was done in the previous Stopper Knot.

Golden Plover in Nara Inlet 9 May '93

**Ankle Bracelet**

In the old sailing ship days it was the custom for seasoned mariners to weave a small turk's-head around their left ankle, and woe betide the greenhorn who dared to do the same! Once on the Turk's-head could not be removed without undoing it, and it might stay there for years.

While on the *Golden Plover* I noticed that the skipper and the mate wore only simple ones, so I plaited some traditional ones out of small cord.

To begin you form up an ordinary 3 part 5 bight Turk's-head. This is then made large enough to be able to fit over the foot. Now you extend the knot as shown until you have around 14 bights. Once you begin you will find that it is quite easy to extend it as long as you wish (for instance it could be made long enough for a hat band).

The end can then be taken around once more, following the course of the original pattern, and this can be done two or three times as desired.

It is then placed on the ankle and gradually worked tight, then the ends are trimmed off flush.

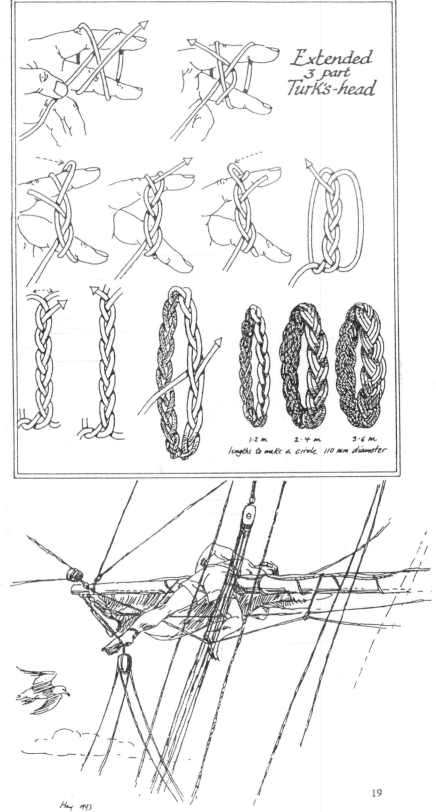

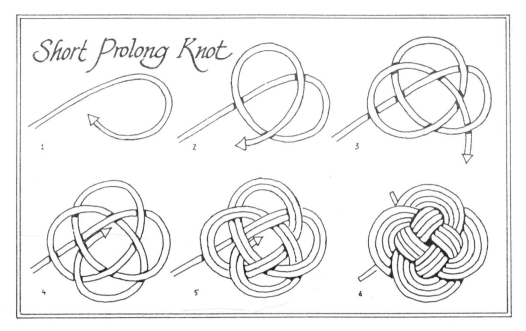

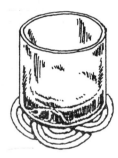

**A Glass Coaster**
**Short Prolong Knot**

This coaster looks good but is not quite as practical as it appears, for it is slightly thicker in the centre than on the edges and so can only be used safely with short, wide glasses. However it certainly adds a nautical touch to a bar.

The Prolong Knot is usually used for mats and is extended to form a roughly rectangular shape, but in this case it is made in its most simple form to form a circle. If you wish to make a mat then the instructions may be found in *Bushcraft 3* page 98. The coaster begins in the same way, as shown in the first three drawings, and then a final loop is put into it as shown in fig.4. The end is then taken around following the original shape as shown in fig.5

This can be done once again, to make 3 parallel strands, or 4 times as shown in fig.6 The ends are then trimmed off so that they are out of sight.

**Amount needed.** More than you would think. 2 metres of 3.17mm diameter venetian blind cord will make a mat only 67mm in diameter. Thicker cord will make a wider mat, but the problem is that it then becomes a bit bulky in the centre.

**3 Part 5 Bight Turk's-head**

This has already been illustrated in the instructions for the ditty bag lanyard. If you take this Turk's-head and flatten it out it can also be used for a mat or a coaster.

3 part 5 bight Turk's-head when flattened

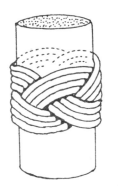

3 part 4 bight Turk's-head

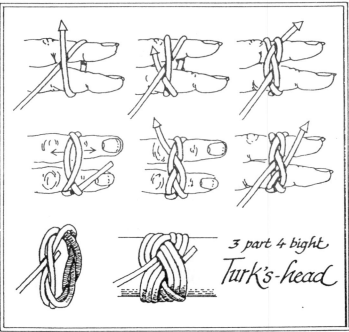

**3 Part 4 Bight Turk's-head**

If you take the coaster that has been made with the Prolong Knot and form it around a cylindrical object it will turn into a Turk's-head like the one shown here.

Like the 3 part 5 bight Turk's-head this one can also be formed on the fingers, and you may find this an interesting way to do it. This is a popular knob cover for whip handles and is also illustrated in *More Bush Leatherwork* page 187, where it is shown being formed around the knob of a whip.

**Carrick Bend**

I have mixed feelings about the carrick bend but am including it because it is an old and widely known knot, and it is attractive because of its symmetrical shape. Speaking of it Ashley says it is "perhaps the nearest thing we have to a perfect bend. It is symmetrical, easy to tie, does not slip easily in wet material, is among the strongest of knots, it cannot jam and is easily untied. To offset this is the sole objection that it is somewhat bulky. It is the bend commonly tied in hawsers and cables."

However a modern writer Floris Hin (The Colour Book of Knots p.35) seems to disagree and says that it will only hold when the knot is stopped, as I have shown in the final sketch. Perhaps this refers only to slippery synthetic ropes, or perhaps the writer was confusing it with some other versions of the bend which Ashley condemns (see Ashley p.263).

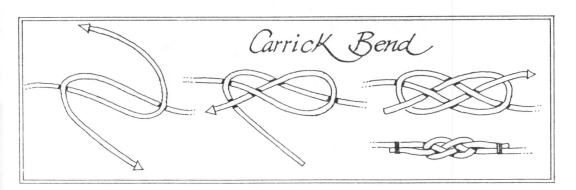

### The Star Knot

The star knot is another of those that Ashley said merited the respect of old time seamen to any of their number who could tie it. From this you will realise that it is not any easy knot to tie, or rather that it is easy enough to tie but difficult to remember (and also to describe). What none of the authorities seem to add is that it is also difficult to tighten up due to the twists that are put into it as it is tied. It cannot be tightened as you go along because of the way the ends have to be fed through the knot towards the end.

I have shown it tied with three strands, but the same method can be used with any number of strands. For instance it looks quite good with four strands, as shown here, and very attractive with five (which I have not illustrated). But by the time you get up to eight strands it becomes too fussy, as you will see from the sketch.

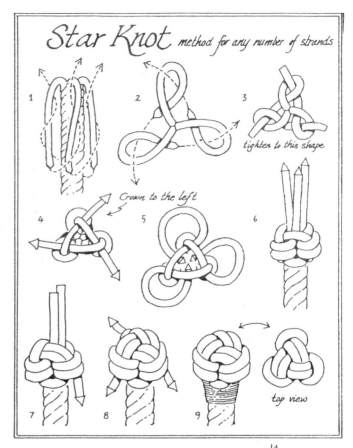

When finished the ends can be whipped to keep them in place or, if you are using synthetic rope, you can probably cut them off flush and then heat them so that they fuse in with the rest of the knot and cannot be removed.

### Becket

Beckets were used on ships for suspending and securing objects. They were not used for heavy weights, and it was important that the knot that acted as the button was large enough and of the right shape not to slip. The Mathew Walker Knot, shown earlier, was a popular one for this purpose, but other stopper knots could be used.

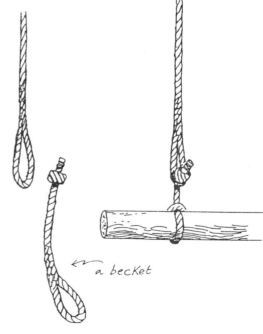

## Ringbolt Hitching or Cockscombing

This type of hitching is today usually referred to as cockscombing, but Ashley in his *Book of Knots* of 1944 called it Ringbolt Hitching and described cockscombing as a "picturesque needlework term" which had been recently applied. Be that as it may the name has now stuck. In its most common form it is done with three strands as illustrated. The method is simple and the end result neat. This hitching got its original name because it was used to cover metal ringbolts on ship's decks and so stop them banging and damaging the deck timbers.

When done on a ring the raised ridge is kept on the outer edge. On a ship the finished work was generally given several coats of white paint, and if done properly made a waterproof covering.

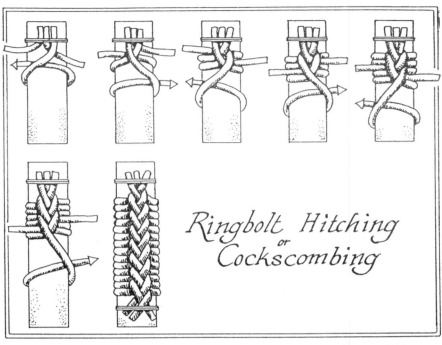

### Single Strand Ringbolt Hitching or Cockscombing

A similar effect to the previous hitching can be obtained with only a single strand, however if you look at the drawings of the finished sections you will notice that there are slight differences in the Vs in the raised section.

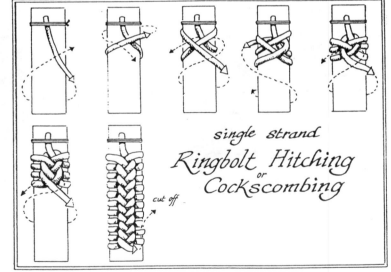

This method is slower than the previous one and if done in cord there is a chance of gaps forming between the horizontal strands. It is also a little more difficult to work it tight. For some reason these problems do not seem to arise when doing this hitch with kangaroo lacing, and the hitches can be worked tight as you go, though you will need a firmly attached needle if you are going to do it this way

**Thump Mat**

Thump mats are aptly named, their purpose is to deaden the sound of fittings thumping on the deck of a boat, and also to save wear and damage to the deck timbers. They are placed wherever necessary, and in the sketch that I did aboard the topsail schooner *One and All* you will see a thump mat roughly indicated at either end of the rail on the deck behind the helmsman's legs. They are most often found where a ringbolt is placed in the deck.

For the person who does not want to bother learning any new knots the easiest way to make a thump mat is to form whatever Turk's-head you might know and then flatten this into a mat. The 3 part, 5 bight Turk's-head is popular for this purpose.

However the knot shown here is even better because it is designed to be a flat knot, and you will notice that it has 6 bights on the outside but only 3 in the centre. I think it would also make a better glass coaster than the one that I have illustrated a few pages earlier.

Ashley illustrates this knot as #2360, but does not explain how to form it, nor does he give it a name other than to note that "it would make a good thump mat for a sheet or traveller block".

It can be tied flat as illustrated, but if you wanted to make a number of them there is a faster way to form the first four steps. Wrap the cord around your fingers, or some other object, three times and then tuck the working end under the top of the first loop. If you now carefully spread out the cord you will find that it will form the shape shown in the fourth drawing. It now only requires an under-over sequence through the centre as shown in the 5th and 6th drawings to complete the knot.

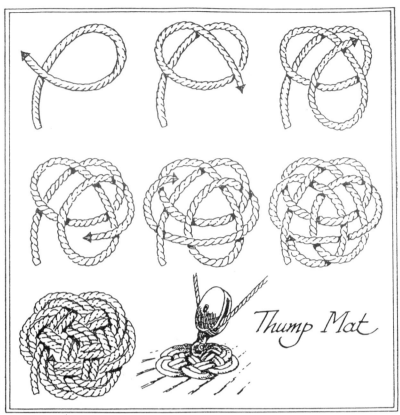

Thump Mat

After it has been formed the working end can be taken around once more to get the effect shown in the 7th drawing, or it can be taken around even more to get a 3 strand effect. Trim off neat and secure the ends with some fine cord or stitching so that it will not come undone.

**Rope Mat using Prolong Knot**

These mats used to be a feature on sailing ships, and they are still found today on well cared for craft. They are not hard to make, but they do take time and also a lot more rope than you would expect. It used to be normal to make these mats from rope which had been used in the rigging and discarded as too worn. This meant that something useful could be made from material that would otherwise be discarded, and it also provided something to do during quiet watches on board. I have already described the making of these mats in *Bushcraft 3* page 98, but have added a little more information here about how to speed up the job.

Form three circles as shown in the first three drawings. Now gently pull the outer ones and fold them over as shown in drawings 4, 5, 6.

The ends of the rope are then interweaved through and the basic shape is complete. The end of the rope is then worked through again to fill up the spaces, and this can be done any number of times. I have shown it done 3 times in the final sketch.

*Rope Mat made with prolong knot*

### Extending the Prolong Knot

It is a simple matter to make this mat longer if desired. When you get to step 4 in the previous diagram you extend the sides even longer. The ends are then folded as shown in steps 5 and 6, and folded again as shown here. The ends of the rope are interwoven through as explained earlier and then the strands are doubled or tripled.

For an even longer mat the ends are folded as often as desired.

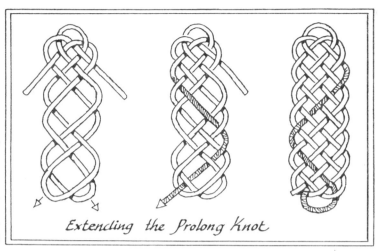

*Extending the Prolong Knot*

### Enlarging a Rope Mat Quickly

As I said earlier this mat takes time to form, especially if you wish to make a large one. One way to speed up the job and produce a most attractive looking mat is to form the centre section of the mat as explained earlier, but use less than half the rope to do this, and leave the rest sitting on the deck untouched.

The remaining rope is now simply wrapped around as shown. Using a needle and thread, the strands are then sewn together, and the mat is turned over so that the stitches are not seen. If the stitches are taken through the centre of the rope they will be out of sight and will not wear.

## GENERAL KNOTS

Many of the previous pages deal with knots that have a decorative function as well as a useful one. This final section deals with everyday knots.

### Thumb Knot

Surely the most simple of knots, it is put into the end of a rope to provide a hand hold or to stop it slipping through a hole.

### Figure of Eight

When a bulkier knot than the thumb knot is needed on the end of a rope the figure of eight will often do the job.

In the sailing ship days this would have been considered only a temporary measure, and a proper stopper knot, such as a Mathew Walker, would have been used.

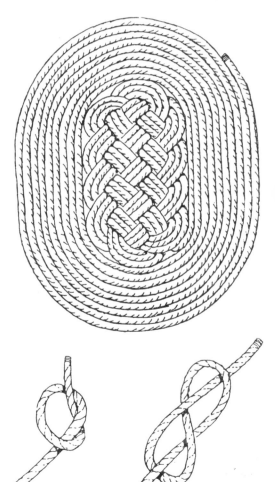

THUMB KNOT     FIGURE OF EIGHT

## Reef Knot

The reef knot is well known, and is used for a wide variety of jobs. It should only be used for joining ropes of the same type and thickness. If you tie the upper section the wrong way round it becomes a Granny Knot, which still works but will gain you no credit.

Ashley did not think much of the reef knot as a method of joining two ropes and gloomily observed (p.18) "The reef knot is probably responsible for more deaths and injuries than have been caused by the failure of all other knots combined."

## Sheet Bend

The sheet bend is more secure than the reef knot and is a good knot for tying together two ropes of different thicknesses.

Whipmaker's will recognize it as being almost the same knot as is used to fix the cracker to the fall, the only difference being that the end of the cracker is a fixed loop.

## Fisherman's Knot

Also known as the Waterman's Knot, and by a few other names. Ashley (p.273) published a list of knots in order of their security according to tests done by jerking the rope and found that this knot is stronger than the sheet bend, and that in turn is stronger than the reef knot. He notes however that this is a bulky knot.

**Timber Hitch**
Fast to form and easy to untie, we use this when dragging logs around with the tractor.

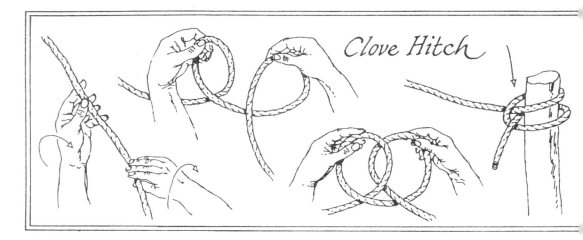

### Clove Hitch

A common knot and easy to tie, but not so stable under pressure combined with movement. It is good for a variety of jobs, but if you wish to hold something tight and under pressure use the **constrictor knot** which is shown next.

The upper drawings show how to form it quickly by twisting and looping to form a pair of circles that can be dropped over a pole. The lower drawing shows how to tie it directly around a pole.

### Constrictor Knot

The constrictor knot is a most useful knot, but one that is still little known. It is used to tightly secure something, can be pulled very tight and holds much firmer than is the case with other knots such as the clove hitch

It appears to be a knot of this century, either invented or evolved by Clifford Ashley, although he does not claim its invention in his *Ashley Book of Knots* but only states (page 225) that he had first tied it 25 years before (c.1919), and that before that time there was no knot that would conveniently secure a bunch of strands when forming sinnets.

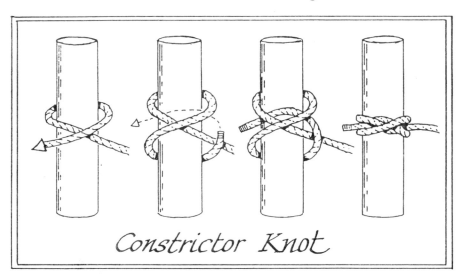

**Sheepshank**

When I was about 12 I was taught this knot and told that it was used for shortening ropes. At the time I could not see any reason for this knot, reasoning that if you wanted a short piece of rope you simply got a long piece and shortened it.

However as I got older I began to find a use for this knot, particularly when shortening guy ropes for tents and other odd jobs, and so I still keep it on my list of useful knots.

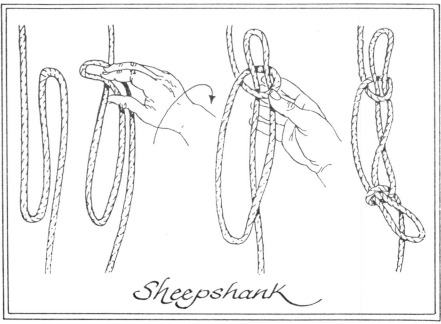

Sheepshank

**Carrier's Knot**

There are several versions of this knot, including one based on the sheepshank given above, but the one illustrated here is probably the most common. It is used to tighten and secure a rope over a load.

Although only one knot is needed for

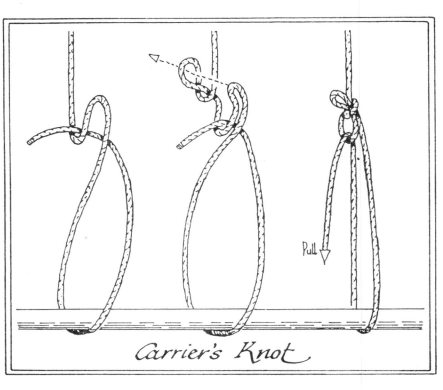

Carrier's Knot

most work it is possible to make a series of them, one pulling on the next, and this increases the amount of pressure that can be put on the rope. Sometimes when erecting a tarp between two trees we apply a number of hitches as shown in the sketch in order to get the rope as tight as possible and reduce the sag.

### Two Half Hitches

There is an old sailor's saying "Two half hitches held the Queen's Ship", and this simple knot is certainly useful for certain jobs. We once had a pair of horses that were tethered out daily for ten years, and this was the only knot that we ever used. In all that time it did not ever come undone.

When I was a kid I was taught a variation of this called *A Round Turn and Two Half Hitches*. This was almost the same knot except that the end of the rope was taken around the pole for one more turn before the hitches were formed in it.

### Ladder Hitch

This is a quick method of forming a loop in a length of rope without having to touch either end. I don't have any need for rope ladders and yet this is a hitch that I use a lot for all sorts of odd jobs.

### Ring Hitch

A simple and well known hitch. If pressure is going to be applied to the rope it should be to both ends. If only one end is pulled the hitch can slip.

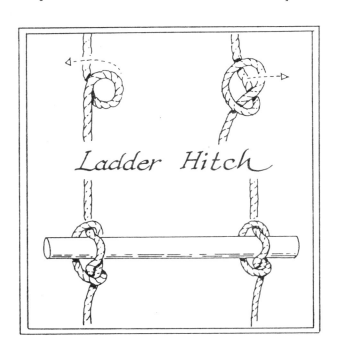

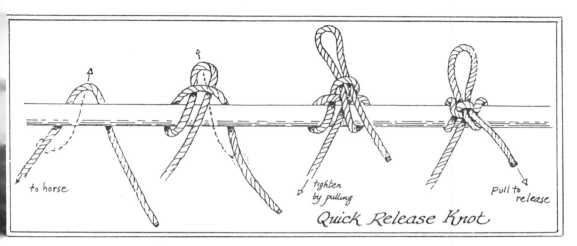

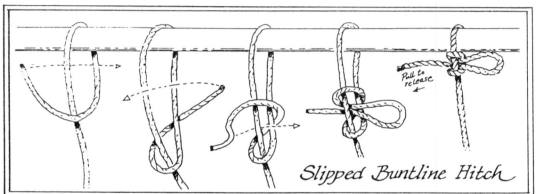

### Quick Release Knot

There are a number of quick release knots, mostly designed for tethering horses to a rail. The idea is that they will keep the horse tied up until the free end is pulled, which causes the knot to fall apart.

These knots should be tied with care, and this is not recommended as a knot for use in climbing.

### Slipped Buntline Hitch

This is another knot that can be used for tying up horses. If you need a knot on which to put your own weight, but one that can later be released from below, this is a better knot than the previous one. However always test it well first, and this advice applies to any knot that is going to be used for serious work.

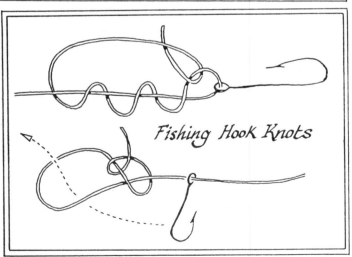

### Fishing Hook Knots

There are many knots designed to fix a hook to a line, these are just a couple that are popular. There are others that are equally as good.

**Mesh Knot**

This is the common knot used for making fishing nets. The making of cast nets is described in *Bushcraft 1* and the making of long nets and how to hang them in *Bushcraft 2*..

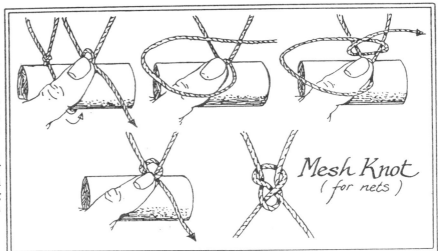

Mesh Knot (for nets)

**Bowline**

This is one of the most useful knots, and well worth learning. The sketch shows a quick way to form it by twisting the rope and so forming a loop. When I was a kid we used to memorise this one by saying "The snake comes out of its hole, around the tree, and back into the hole".

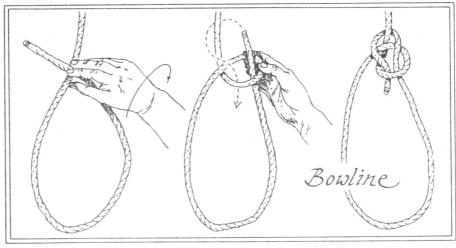

Bowline

**Honda Knot**

This is a rather specialised knot, used to form the loop in a lasso. Unlike the bowline, in which the end hangs down inside the loop, this leaves the centre of the loop clear and so allows the rope to run through easily.

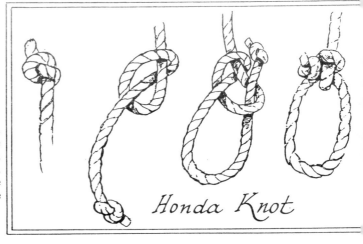

Honda Knot

**Hangman's Noose**
I think that all kids learn this knot, at least they all did when I was a child. Apart from its macabre interest it is not a great deal of use.

**Common Whipping**
Whipping is put on the ends of rope to stop it unravelling. This is the most common form, but many seafarers do not like it because it can come loose if the rope flicks around a lot, or if it is roughly handled.

**Long Whipping**
This is a stronger form of whipping than the common one, and is the one often used to attach keepers to whip handles.

Wrap the twine a little more than half way, form a loop and continue wrapping loosely. After a number of turns have been done stick the end up as shown and then wind the twine as tight as you can. Pull up the end, and cut it off flush.

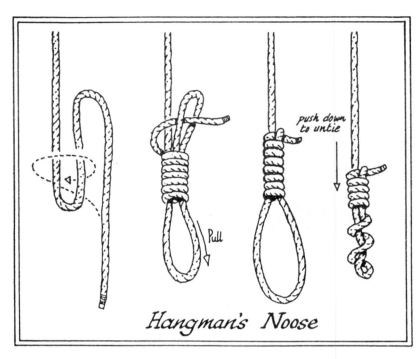

*Hangman's Noose*

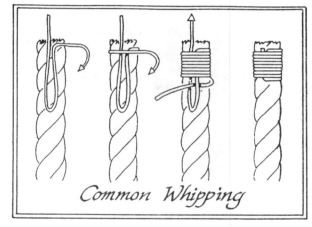

*Common Whipping*

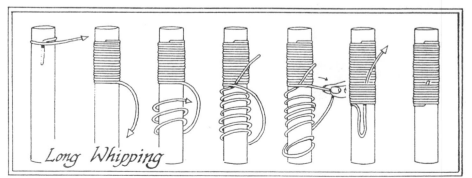

*Long Whipping*

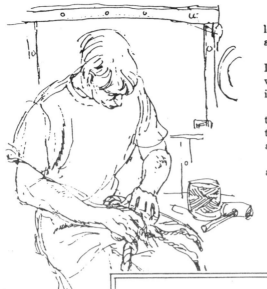

lower one. Finally the rope was turned around and upper strand was put in the back.

However once I sat down and tried doing it I realised that it was just a more complicated way of doing the same thing that I have illustrated here

Once the three strands are in place they are then simply worked up the rope, beginning with the lower strand each time and tucking it over and under.

For a neater job the rope ends can be tapered as they go up.

**EYE SPLICE**

In *Bushcraft 1*, p.124, *Bushcraft 2*, p.59 and *Bushcraft 3*, p.94 I illustrated methods of forming an eye splice, but while sailing on the *One and All* in September 1993 I was shown another beginning and was assured that it was the best. The sketch shows John Richardson, one of the crew, putting an eye splice into a stopper.

This splice was formed by first putting in the middle strand, and then the

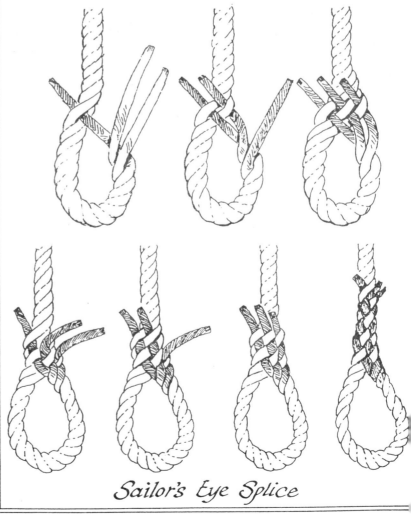

*Sailor's Eye Splice*

## Eye Splice in the Bight

This knot was shown to me by a professional rigger, Graham Foster of Stratford, Qld, and allows you to place an eye splice anywhere along the length of a rope.

The great knotting expert Ashley did not like this knot and said that it was "ruinous to rope", but that was in the days when ropes were made of natural fibre. Modern synthetic ropes do not seem to be so affected and the knot can be untied without leaving any trace in the rope.

*Eye Splice in the Bight*

## Fast Eye Splice

This is a fast way to produce a temporary eye splice in a length of rope. Although it is very simple it holds well, for as pressure is put on the loop the same pressure holds tight the strands that are containing the end of the rope. It is also an easy splice to undo. However it is nowhere near as strong as a proper eye splice, and certainly looks like a makeshift.

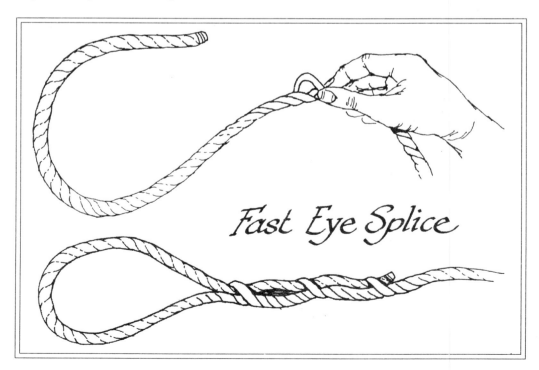

*Fast Eye Splice*

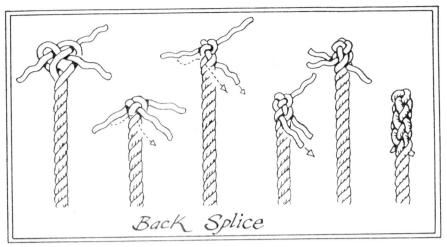

## Back Splice

This splice can be used to finish off a length of rope and stop it unravelling. It is not as common as a whipping on the end of a rope, and yet it only takes about the same time to do, and the effect is permanent.

First tie a crown knot in the end of the rope, then take each strand in turn and work them in as shown.

## Common Splice

This is used to join two ropes together. Make sure you do a good long splice if there is going to be a lot of pressure put on the rope.

The method is simple and easy. Unwind the rope ends for a little way and then push both together. If you have not done this sort of work before you will find it helps to put a temporary tie in the middle while you are doing the first half of the job. Remove it before doing the second half. After you have done a few splices this tie will not be needed.

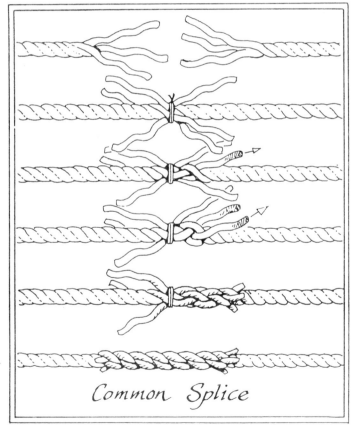

The ends are just tucked in as shown, one after the other, until all the strands have been used up.